GROW IT
EAT IT

DK

LONDON, NEW YORK,
MELBOURNE, MUNICH, and DELHI

This edition published 2009 for Index Books Ltd.

Senior designer Sonia Whillock-Moore
Senior editor Deborah Lock
Designers Sadie Thomas, Rachael Smith, Gemma Fletcher
Photography Will Heap
Food stylist Annie Nichols
RHS consultant Simon Maughan
Food consultant Jill Bloomfield

Category publisher Mary Ling
Production editor Clare McLean
Production controller Claire Pearson
Jacket designers Sonia Whillock-Moore, Sadie Thomas
Jacket editor Mariza O'Keeffe
Jacket copywriter Adam Powley

First published in Great Britain in 2008 by
Dorling Kindersley Limited, 80 Strand, London, WC2R 0RL
in association with The Royal Horticultural Society
www.rhs.org.uk
Foreword copyright © 2008 Jill Bloomfield
This edition published 2010 for Index Books Ltd.

Copyright © 2008 Dorling Kindersley Limited
A Penguin Company
2 4 6 8 10 9 7 5 3 1
GD103 – 02/08

A CIP catalogue record for this book
is available from the British Library
ISBN 978-1-40535-756-2

Colour reproduction by MDP, UK
Printed and bound by Toppan, China

Discover more at
www.dk.com

Contents

● 4-5   Know it: Green-fingered gardener

● 6-7   Know it: Pots and plots

● 8-9   Know it: Labels and markers

● 10-11   Know it: From seed to seedling

● 12-13   Know it: From flower to fruit

● 14-15   Know it: Recycle and renew

● 16-17   Eat it: Kitchen know-how

● 18-19   Grow it: Tomato

● 20-21   Grow it: Aubergine

● 22-23   Eat it: Tomato and aubergine towers

● 24-25   Grow it: Courgette

● 26-27   Eat it: Courgette frittata

● 28-29   Grow it: Pumpkin

● 30-31   Eat it: Mini pumpkin pies

● 32-33   Grow it: Beans

● 34-35   Eat it: Giant beanstalk stir-fry

● 36-37   Grow it: Potato

● 38-39   Eat it: Mashed potato fishcakes

● 40-41   Grow it: Onion and leek

- 42-43 Eat it: Onion and leek soup
- 44-45 Grow it: Carrots
- 46-47 Eat it: Carrot and orange muffins
- 48-49 Grow it: Spinach and beetroot
- 50-51 Eat it: Green leaf tarts
- 52-53 Grow it: Lettuce
- 54-55 Eat it: Rainbow salad
- 56-57 Grow it: Mint
- 58-59 Eat it: Chocolate and mint mousse
- 60-61 Grow it: Sunflower
- 62-63 Eat it: Sunflower pot loaves
- 64-65 Grow it: Strawberries
- 66-67 Eat it: Strawberry meringue
- 68-69 Grow it: Blueberries
- 70-71 Eat it: Blueberry cheesecake
- 72-73 Grow it: Lemon
- 74-75 Eat it: Lemonade lollies
- 76-77 Know it: Collecting seeds
- 78-79 Eat it: More recipe ideas
- 80 Index and Acknowledgements

Get involved

Become an **RHS Garden Explorer** and get digging and discovering with the experts. Membership of Garden Explorers allows families and children to access RHS Gardens for free all year, as well as having exclusive access to events and days out - including trails, gardening activity packs and masses of family-friendly fun.

For more information and to join, please contact:
RHS Garden Explorers,
PO Box 313, London
SW1P 2PE.
Tel. 0845 130 4646
www.rhs.org.uk/explorers

Foreword

Growing your own fruits and vegetables is easy and fun. Imagine growing a pumpkin of your very own or a bunch of bright orange carrots. With tending and patience, a seed you sow will become a tiny green seedling poking out of the soil. By watering and feeding your plant, it will become strong and bear blossoms and leaves. The plant will bud tiny fruits or vegetables that will grow bigger and bigger before your eyes. Imagine how much fun harvesting your fruits and vegetables will be!

You can share your harvest with others by cooking these yummy recipes. Eating blueberry cheesecake in summer and pumpkin pies in autumn reminds us that the freshest, healthiest, and tastiest food is grown right in your own garden! So, get ready to plan your plot to grow the amazing ingredients you need to cook up a feast for family and friends.

Jill Bloomfield

Whatever you decide to grow, caring for your plants is the key to becoming a "green-fingered" gardener. Thinking about what your plants need will help you choose what tools and equipment you need to have.

Remember to wear old clothes because you'll be getting your hands dirty! You'll also need boots or shoes you don't mind getting dirty.

Trial and error is the way many gardeners learn. Finding out what works and what doesn't is part of the fun of gardening.

Light

Plants need the Sun's warmth but also protection from wind and rain. Find suitable places for growing your plants inside and outside. You need pots and containers or a small garden patch to grow your plants in. See page 6.

Grow-it symbols

A sunny or slightly shaded place

A warm, sheltered, sunny place

A place with direct sunlight

4

Soil

Plants need good soil that provides grip for the roots, prevents water draining away, and is filled with nutrients (goodness) for healthy growing. You need a hand trowel, hand fork, and small rake to prepare the soil for plants. A wheelbarrow is useful, too.

Compost adds goodness to the soil.

See page 14 for tips on how to make your own rich, crumbly compost.

Water

Plants need water to make their food, but some plants need less water than others. Water in the soil is drawn up by the roots and transported to the leaves through the stem. Also, spraying some plants with water helps their fruit to set. You need a watering can and a spray.

Support

Some plants need support as they grow tall, since their stems have to support the weight of the fruit. You need canes and twine.

Cover the top of your cane to protect your eyes.

Support your large fruit in hammocks made from the netting of an orange bag.

Protection

Plants need protecting from some garden bugs and diseases. There are many creatures that eat the pests, such as birds and ladybirds, which eat aphids. Strong-scented herbs may drive away any pests with their smell. Also try companion planting – see pages 19 and 45.

Protect young plants from hungry slugs and snails by putting them on a table top. Use eggshells around the plants as well.

Use netting to stop birds eating the fruit.

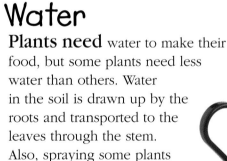

You'll need pots and containers in all shapes and sizes depending on what you decide to grow. Pots also keep plants healthy throughout their growing stages.

Small pots

Small pots for sowing seeds need to be between 5 cm (2 in) and 7.5 cm (3 in) deep. Start a collection of yoghurt and mousse pots, tubs, and tins. They can all be re-used as pots.

Pots and more pots
Transform your balcony or garden patio by growing plants in pots of all shapes, sizes, and colours.

Lollipop sticks can be used as labels

Empty yoghurt pots that have been washed out well

Biodegradable egg boxes that will rot away when put directly into soil

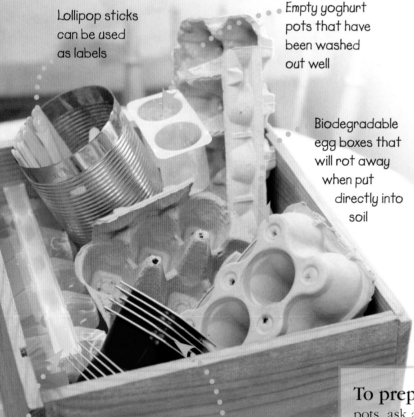

A plastic egg box can become a mini greenhouse

Empty mousse pots that have been cleaned well

Odd pots

Re-use ice-cream tubs to plant seeds and use the lids as drip trays.

Cut the top off a large plastic container and it becomes a pot.

To prepare small pots, ask an adult to make a couple of holes in the bottom for drainage, using a pair of scissors or something similar with a sharp point. Fill the pot with rich seedling compost ready to sow your seeds.

Large pots

Medium pots between 12 cm (5 in) and 15 cm (6 in) across are needed for transplanting seedlings that have outgrown their sowing pot, but are not yet ready to be kept outside all the time.

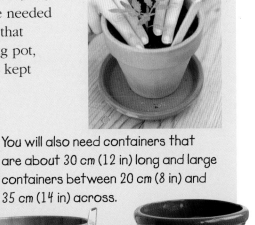

You will also need containers that are about 30 cm (12 in) long and large containers between 20 cm (8 in) and 35 cm (14 in) across.

Potatoes in tyres

Washing bowls, old boots, or even old drawers make unusual plant containers. Line them with a waterproof plastic sheet, punch out a few small holes, and they're ready to use.

If you have the space, you could grow your plants in your own garden patch. Make a small raised bed so that you don't step on the soil to get to your plants.

Preparing pots

1 **Ask an adult** to make some holes in the bottom of the container if there are none.

2 **Place some crock** (pieces of broken pots) or large stones over the holes. These will prevent the soil from draining away when you are watering.

3 **Fill the container** with rich soil ready for a plant.

Know it Labels and markers

As you plant your seeds, remember to add a label. When seedlings appear, it can get very confusing to identify which plant is which. Your labels can be as simple as lollipop sticks with names written on them, or you can have some fun making and decorating your own.

Some vegetables and fruits have many varieties and each one will be different. Look out for the variety on the seed packet and include it on your label.

Stone markers

Mark the pots that you have used with colourful stones. What eye-catching designs will you paint on?

Why not paint a stone in one colour and then choose another colour for a flower or the first letter of your name?

Paint

Tall labels

Labels on sticks will stand out in a pot. They are ideal markers for plants that will grow tall and bushy, such as herbs. Waterproof labels can be made using pizza bases, which are also easy to cut and paint.

You will need:

Kebab sticks

Recycle a pizza base

Re-use an old plastic bottle

1. Carefully cut off the base of your bottle.

2. Cut a small circle out of your pizza base...

3. Push your stick inside the circle and glue to the bottle base.

4. Now decorate your flower.

Basil

Butterfly

1. Draw a butterfly on a pizza base. Cut it out.

2. Push your stick inside the butterfly. Now it's ready to paint.

Lolly-stick labels

Lolly sticks are very handy as labels for small seed pots. Use pens to draw a picture of the vegetable you have planted or to make a stripy pattern in the same colours as the vegetable.

You can also use a clothes peg to label your seedling.

Paint the end of a lolly stick to measure how deep to make your seed hole.

1 cm (⅓ in)

2 cm (¾ in)

3 cm (1⅓ in)

Leek

9

Know it From seed to seedling

As a gardener, you will be taking care of your plants throughout their life cycles. The growth of a seed into a seedling is called **germination**. Seeds will start germinating if they have enough water, air, and warmth.

Seed leaves are the first ones to appear, but they look different from the plant's true leaves.

The seed contains all the food that the new plant needs to grow.

1 day +

Seed leaves

Seed coat

Food store

2 days +

Seed leaves

Seed roots

The true leaves form after the seed leaves. They have a distinctive shape and this will help you to identify the plant. With leaves, the seedling can now begin to make its own food and grow. This process is called **photosynthesis**. The leaves are where photosynthesis takes place.

True leaves

3-5 days +

Seed leaves

For photosynthesis, plants take carbon dioxide [CO_2] from the air and water from the soil, and use sunlight to join them together to make sugar-based food. Oxygen [O_2] is released as a waste product and humans need this to breathe.

Sunlight

O_2

CO_2

Water

The stem supports the plant and transports water and nutrients from the roots to the leaves.

A week +

Tomatoes, courgettes, and blueberries are just some of the "fruits" of a plant that we eat. But how do plants form these and what can gardeners do to encourage their growth? The answer is found in the secret workings of flowers.

Insects, such as bees, get covered in pollen as they drink from the sweet nectar in the flower. A bee collects pollen on its back legs to take back to the hive.

Flowers are the place where the male and female parts of a plant are found. To form fruits, the male powdery yellow pollen has to reach the female ovules, which are like the eggs. This process is called **pollination.**

While some plants can self-pollinate, others need a bit of help from insects, animals, or the wind to move pollen around from flower to flower.

1 **This tomato plant** has bright yellow flowers for attracting insects. The bee is already covered in pollen from the last tomato flower it visited.

2 **Once the pollen grains** have rubbed off the bee onto the flower's stigma, they travel down to the ovary, or egg chamber where the pollen enters the ovules. Then the fruit starts to grow and the yellow petals fall away.

When tomatoes were first brought to Europe from South America in the 1500s, people thought they were poisonous. Tomato-eating demonstrations were held in market places to prove that they were safe to eat.

3 Sunshine, water, and nutrients from the soil help the tomato to grow bigger and become firm. So, keep watering and using a liquid feed as required.

4 The fruit changes colour and once red and ripe, it is ready for picking. Cut the fruit in half and you will see the seeds that the fleshy part has been protecting. The plant wilts and dies but its seeds might survive to bring new life.

The inside story

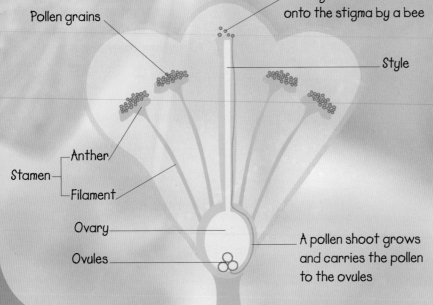

Pollen grains

Pollen grains carried onto the stigma by a bee

Style

Stamen
 —Anther
 —Filament

Ovary

Ovules

A pollen shoot grows and carries the pollen to the ovules

This diagram shows what the inside of a flower looks like if you cut it in half. Most flowers have a long central stem called a **style** with a sticky end called a **stigma**, which catches the pollen grains. Around the style are **stamens**, which have **anthers** covered in the flower's own pollen. If pollen does not land on the stigma, **pollination** cannot happen and the fruit will not grow.

Warning!
Chemical sprays can harm insects. Without insects, most pollination cannot happen. Try to grow your plants organically (without chemicals).

Recycled glass beads or seashells can be used as decorative mulch.

Tomato

Round or plum-shaped, cherry or monster-sized, yellow, orange, green, stripy, or just deep red, there's a load of tomato varieties to grow and try out. Which will be your favourite?

1 **Fill a shallow** container with soil. Scatter the seeds thinly over the surface. Make sure the container has holes in the bottom for drainage.

2 **Cover the seeds** with a thin layer of soil, then water them gently. Add a label, then place the container on a windowsill.

3 **Thin out the seedlings** to allow room for others to continue growing, and developing good roots. Water to keep the soil moist but not too wet.

4 **Once two true leaves** have formed, the seedlings are ready to be put into individual small pots. Be gentle and careful as you place in a seedling.

5 **Once your plant** has grown twice as high as its pot, plant it into a larger pot. Make a hole first, then place in the plant, pat the soil around it, and water.

Put a plastic bottle on the cane to cap the blunt end.

6 **Push in a cane** a little away from the main stem. Use string to tie the stem to the cane.

18

still. Gently mix the ingredients together in a bowl.

folding it over and pressing down with the heel of your hand.

7 **Pinch out** the shoots that appear where the leaves join the stems. Pinch out the growing tip once your plant has four or five flowering stems, or "trusses".

8 **Fine-spray the plant** with water to encourage the fruits to set. Water each day and add liquid feed every week to grow the best fruit.

Red and ripe, ready for picking!

Grow marigolds in the same pot as your tomato plant. These flowers can keep away aphids, which might otherwise infest your tomato plant. This is called companion planting.

19

Aubergine

An aubergine has not always been a dark purple fruit. It's evolved from a spiny plant from India with a small, white egg-shaped fruit. This is why an aubergine is also known as an eggplant.

1 **Fill a pot** with seed compost after making some holes in its base (see page 6). With your fingertips, make a hole about 6 mm (¼ in) deep in the soil.

2 **Sow two seeds** in the hole and gently brush some surrounding soil over with your fingers. Remember to add a label and water. Keep on a windowsill.

3 **After germinating,** remove the weakest seedling to allow the strongest one to continue growing and developing good roots.

4 **Make a hole** in the soil in a large container. Carefully, tip the young plant out of its pot and place into the hole. Pat the soil around it and water in.

5 **Water little but often** as aubergine plants don't like their soil too wet or too dry. If you have a greenhouse, your plant will flourish there.

6 **Look out for flowers.** These have five petals with a yellow centre. They are very colourful to attract insects for pollinating.

7 Spray the new fruits that develop from the flowers with water. As the fruits start to swell, add liquid feed each time you water.

8 Pinch out the growing tips once the plant has grown to 30 cm (12 in). You may want to tie your plant to a cane for added support.

Cut each fruit with scissors when it is more than 10 cm (4 in) long and still has a shine on its skin. You might get between five and ten fruits over a few months.

Eat it Tomato and aubergine towers

Aubergines and slow-roasted tomatoes are so easy to prepare and burst with flavour. They can be used in salads, soups, bruschetta, and sauces.

You'll need

6 large ripe tomatoes, cut in half	2 garlic cloves, finely chopped	1 tbsp dried oregano	8 tbsp extra-virgin olive oil	sea salt and freshly ground black pepper	1 large aubergine *thinly sliced*	pinch of smoked paprika	8 tbsp of natural yoghurt	2 tbsp of runny honey	4 tbsp toasted blanched almonds *chopped roughly*	Pre-heat 150°C, 275°F. Gas 3

1 Lay the tomatoes cut-side up on a baking tray. Mix the garlic and oregano with the salt, pepper, and half the olive oil. Spoon this over the tomatoes.

2 Bake in the oven. Check the tomatoes every now and then. When ready, they should be slightly shrunk, but still a brilliant red colour. Allow to cool.

Baking time 3–4 hours

3 Layer the slices of aubergine in a colander, sprinkling a little salt between each layer. Leave for 30 minutes then rinse well with water and dry.

Tomatoes can be eaten straight after picking. Go on try one!

4 Place the aubergine slices in a large bowl, pour over the rest of the olive oil, and sprinkle with a little paprika. Toss together with your hands.

Cooking time 2–3 mins

5 Heat a ridged griddle pan, then add a single layer of the aubergine slices. Cook each side until tender. Place the slices on a plate. Repeat for the other slices.

Pour on some honey and sprinkle with chopped almonds.

Go to page 78 for more tomato and aubergine recipe ideas.

6 **To serve, create** towers by piling up the aubergine slices and tomato halves in alternate layers. Drizzle two tablespoons of yoghurt over each tower.

Courgette

As a member of the squash family, courgette plants can grow very large. Each year, why not choose a different variety as courgettes can be many odd shapes, colours, and sizes?

1 Push two seeds on their sides down into a 1.5 cm (½ in) deep hole in a small pot filled with soil. Water well, label, and put the pot on a windowsill.

2 Remove the weakest seedling and put the strong one outside during the daytime. Cover the plant with part of a plastic bottle for protection.

3 When the roots begin to show through the bottom of the pot, the plant is ready to place into the ground or a big container. Dig out a hole.

5 Look out for the bright yellow male and female flowers. They open up to attract insects, which will pass pollen from the male to the female flowers.

6 Water the soil around the plant and not over it, as this could cause rotting. Keep the soil moist. Use a liquid feed to encourage more fruit to grow.

7 Pick off the female flower from the tip of the growing courgette. These can be cooked and eaten. If left on, they will shrivel and drop off by themselves.

Planting in pots

Courgette plants will thrive in pots, especially if kept well fed and watered. You could bury a small pot into the soil next to your plant. Water into this, so the water flows to the roots of the plant.

4 Tip the young plant out of its pot, carefully supporting it at the base of its stem. Place it in the hole, fill gaps with soil, pat around it, and water.

8 Cut the courgettes at their base when they reach 10 cm (4 in) long. Ask an adult to help as a sharp knife needs to be used for cutting.

Courgettes are young marrows, so you might choose to leave a few attached to grow twice as long to become large marrows.

Courgette frittata

Ciao! This recipe is not just an ordinary omelette, but an Italian one filled with your home-grown vegetables. Buon appetito! (Have a good meal!)

You'll need

500 g (18 oz) new potatoes

50 g (2 oz) butter

1 large onion, finely chopped

3 courgettes, thinly sliced

1 tbsp fresh mint leaves, chopped

8 eggs

finely grated

75 g (3 oz) Pecorino cheese

a pinch of ground black pepper

1 **Cook the potatoes** in boiling water for 15-20 minutes or until tender. Use a colander to drain them. Let them cool down, and then halve if large.

Cooking time 5 mins

2 **Melt the butter** in a 28 cm (11 in) diameter, non-stick frying pan. Add the onion and cook gently until soft. Add the courgettes and cook. Stir often.

Cooking time 5 mins

3 **Stir in the potatoes** and continue cooking for a further five minutes, until the courgettes have softened.

4 **Crack the eggs** into a bowl and add the Pecorino and mint and season well with pepper. Whisk together well using a fork.

Cooking time 5 mins

5 **Pour the egg** mixture into the pan and turn the heat down as low as possible.

Cooking time 5 mins

6 **When the eggs** are just set, place the pan under a pre-heated grill to brown the top. When ready, remove from the grill and leave the frittata to cool.

Go to page 78 for another courgette recipe idea.

A brilliant dish for picnics!

Grow pumpkins in a sunny, sheltered place.

Pumpkin

These large, heavy fruits belong to the squash family. Pumpkins take a long time to ripen, but other varieties of summer squash will grow quicker. The hard, inedible skins make these fruits ideal for storing.

1 In spring, fill a pot with soil and make a 1.5 cm (½ in) deep hole. Sow one seed on its side into the hole, cover with soil, and water. Put on a windowsill.

2 Keep well watered after germination. Your plant will be ready to transplant once the roots begin to show through the bottom of the pot.

3 Make a pot-sized hole in a large, deep container. Carefully place the plant into the hole. Pat around the base to make sure the plant is upright. Water.

5 Keep the soil well watered. Your plant will produce male and female flowers, attracting insects to visit both to pollinate.

6 Feed your plant with a suitable plant food every few weeks once the fruits start to form in the female flowers. The flowers will now shrivel and drop off.

7 Make a hammock out of netting to support any fruit growing above the ground. Attach the ends of the hammock to the canes.

Once it has reached 60 cm (2 ft), the growing tip should be broken off so the plant can redirect goodness to its fruit.

Native Americans not only used pumpkins for savoury and dessert dishes, but also wove dried strips of pumpkin into mats.

4 **Push four canes** into the pot and wrap the stem around them. Tie the stem to the canes with string. As the stem grows longer, continue to wrap it around the canes and tie up.

8 **Add mulch** around fruit growing on the ground to cushion it. Keep turning the fruit slightly so the colour ripens evenly. The leaves will now start dying.

9 **Cut** the fruit once it has fully matured. Ask an adult to help you cut it and lift it.

Eat it Mini pumpkin pies

You'll need

Ask an adult to cut the pumpkin in half with a sharp knife, using a rocking motion. Scoop out the seeds. Slice the pumpkin into pieces, and cut off the skin.

Pre-heat

peeled, deseeded

cut into 16 pieces

500 g (18 oz) pumpkin, cut into large chunks	1 tbsp olive oil	375 g (15 oz) puff pastry	1 tbsp plain flour	90 g (3 oz) treacle	1 whole egg	3 large egg yolks	300 ml (11 fl oz) milk	½ a split vanilla pod	a pinch of salt	190°C, 375°F, Gas 5

Roasting time

30–35 mins

1 **On a baking tray,** pour olive oil over the pumpkin pieces. Evenly coat them, using your hands. Roast until tender. Cool and then mash with a fork.

Refrigerate for 30 mins

2 **Shape the puff pastry** pieces into balls. Roll out each ball until about 6 cm (2½ in) diameter. Press each piece into a bun tin and put into the fridge.

Handy tip!

Baking time

15 mins

3 **Place a piece of** parchment paper into each pastry and fill to the top with baking beans. Bake in the oven then remove the paper and beans.

4 **Pour the milk** into a pan. Scrape out the vanilla seeds from the pod and add to the milk. Heat the mixture until just below boiling point. Leave to cool a little.

5 **Lightly beat** the egg yolks, whole egg, and treacle in a bowl. Add the flour and salt and beat until smooth. Strain the hot milk over the mixture and beat.

6 **Pour the smooth** mixture into a pan and bring to the boil, stirring all the time until thickened. Remove from heat and stir in the pumpkin puree.

30

Go to page 78 for another pumpkin recipe idea.

7 Spoon out

the mixture evenly into the pastry cases. Bake in the oven for 20-25 minutes until just firm and slightly puffed up. Serve the pies warm with a dusting of icing sugar on the top if you wish.

Grow beans in a sunny, sheltered place.

Beans

Runners or french, long or dwarf, you'll have a tough choice deciding which beans to grow. You also have a choice about how to sow your beans. Here are two ways to get started.

Scarlet runner bean flower

Either, plant one bean seed per small pot, or a handful of beans around a large shallow container to get them started. Cover with soil, then water, and label. Once the seedlings have grown their true leaves, transplant them to the base of a cane wigwam structure. Put one or two at the base of each cane.

1 Or, push four canes into a large pot and tie them together at the top to make a wigwam structure.

2 Press the beans about 5 cm (2 in) deep into the soil. Plant one on each side of a cane. Cover with soil and water. Write a label with the bean name.

3 Wind each seedling around its nearest cane, and then it will continue to grow up it. Cover the soil with straw or mulch and protect the plants from slugs.

4 Rub off any aphids you see with your fingers, or squirt them with a spray of water. Keep watering the soil often and use a liquid feed every two weeks.

People have been growing beans for many thousands of years. Since ancient times, beans have been eaten as a good source of protein.

5 Pick the beans when they are long but still young and tender. Pick regularly so that other beans will grow. You could get a crop for the next eight weeks.

Leave a few pods on your plant to dry out, so you can open and re-use the beans inside to grow bean plants next year. See page 76.

 # Giant beanstalk stir-fry

Grab yourself a handful of beans from your beanstalk and be amazed at how quickly you can magic up a stir-fry for any Giant's appetite!

 You'll need

 unsweetened

 core removed

 thinly sliced

 15g (3 oz) unsalted cashew nuts

chopped

50g (2 oz) dessicated coconut	2 tbsp sunflower oil	1 clove of garlic, sliced	6 spring onions, chopped	1 bulb of fennel, sliced	500 g (1 lb) french and runner beans	2 tbsp soy sauce, 1 tbsp rice vinegar	100 g (4 oz) beansprouts	50 g (2 oz) fresh coriander	200 g (8 oz) wholewheat noodles	1 tbsp sesame seeds

1 **Place the coconut** in a bowl of warm water, cover, and leave for 20 minutes. Strain the coconut through a sieve, pressing it against the sides.

2 **Heat the oil** in a large frying pan or wok. Add the garlic, onion, and fennel. Stir all the time for about two minutes, using a wooden spoon.

3 **Add your sliced beans** and fry quickly, stirring all the time. Pour on the soy sauce and vinegar. Stir in, then remove the pan from the heat.

4 **Add the beansprouts** to the stir-fry. Sprinkle on the coconut and coriander. Then give the mixture another good stir. Mmm! Smells good.

5 **Cook some noodles,** following the instructions on the packet. Drain the noodles using a colander, then spoon them into your serving bowls.

6 **Spoon out the stir-fry** on top of the noodles. After roasting the cashew nuts and sesame seeds, sprinkle over and serve. Fee fi fo fum, here I come!

Go to page 78 for another bean recipe idea.

Crunchy, nutty beans

35

Potato

Slowly growing, hidden from view, potatoes are the enlarged parts of the underground stem of a potato plant. They are called "tubers". Choose from three groups of potatoes – earlies, second earlies, and maincrop – depending on when you want to plant and harvest them.

1 Buy seed potatoes at the end of winter. Lay them out separately with their "eyes" uppermost in a cool, dry, light place or windowsill. They'll take about six weeks to sprout shoots.

2 Make holes in the base of a large container, such as a bin or a large mesh sack. Add some crock, gravel, or stones, and fill the container with a 10 cm (4 in) layer of soil.

3 In spring, once the potatoes have sprouted short shoots, they are ready to plant. Carefully place five potatoes on top of the soil with the shoots facing upwards.

5 Once the shoots re-appear, cover them with more soil so they are just buried. This is called "earthing up". Keep repeating this until the container is full.

6 Keep the soil well watered especially in dry weather. Remove any weeds. Use a general-purpose fertilizer every couple of weeks.

7 Flowering shows that the potatoes have reached a good size, so you could lift some. Early varieties can be lifted as "new potatoes" in early summer.

Keep the potatoes well covered with soil by earthing up as they grow. They will turn green in sunlight. Green potatoes are poisonous.

The ancient Peruvians were the first to grow potatoes. Later, the Incas not only ate them, but also measured time by how long it took to cook them.

4 **Add a little more soil** to cover the potatoes by a further 2.5 cm (1 in) layer.

8 **Otherwise wait** until the leaves die back in autumn. Now, tip over the container and enjoy finding the potatoes buried in the soil. Look carefully.

Eat it Mashed potato fishcakes

You'll need

	unpeeled, boiled and mashed	chopped finely	hard-boiled	chopped	
250 g (10 oz) undyed smoked haddock	1 fresh bay leaf	300 ml (11 fl oz) milk	375 g (15oz) potatoes	8 spring onions	100 g (4oz) sweetcorn kernels	4 eggs	2 tbsp fresh parsley	zest of 1 lemon	8 tbsp double cream

2 egg yolks | 3 tbsp flour | 25 g (1 tbsp) butter | a pinch of freshly ground black pepper | 2 tbsp olive oil | 500 g (1 lb) fresh shelled or frozen peas | a few spoonfuls of mayonnaise | 4 tbsp yoghurt or double cream | handful of cherry tomatoes

Baked in jackets, boiled and mashed, sliced and fried, roasted – these are just a few of the many ideas for cooking your potatoes. They are a healthy energy-providing food. All you have to decide is which way will you cook them today.

Simmering time 5-10 mins

1 Cook the haddock fillets with the bay leaf and the milk in a shallow pan. Cool, then remove the fish's skin and any bones, and flake into chunks.

2 Mix the fish, potato, spring onions, sweetcorn, eggs, parsley, and zest. In a small bowl, beat the cream with the egg yolks, and stir into the mixture.

3 Divide the mixture into four parts. With floured hands, shape each part into a slightly flattened ball. Roll each fishcake in the flour on a plate. Shaking off any excess.

4 Heat the oil and butter in a frying pan and add the fishcakes carefully. Cook them gently for about 4-5 minutes on each side, or until golden brown.

Cooking time 2-3 mins

5 To cook the peas, bring a pan of water to the boil then add the peas. Once cooked, drain away the water, using a colander.

Go to page 78 for more potato recipe ideas.

Jacket-potato mice

Serve with a spoonful of mayonnaise and tomato halves.

6 **Place the peas** in a food processor and blend until smooth. Scrape the squashed peas into a bowl and stir in the yoghurt or cream. Season with black pepper.

Onion

Plants from the onion family all have swollen leaf bases or bulbs. Large onions, spring onions, shallots, leeks, and even garlic are part of this family.

Onions can be grown quicker by planting onion sets.

1 Make a trench 1.5 cm (½ in) deep in a small container. Sow onion seeds very thinly along the row. Cover with soil, then water, and add a label.

2 Alternatively, sow your seeds in biodegradable bags. Do this in early spring or late summer for harvesting later in the year.

3 After they have germinated, thin out the onion seedlings and pull out any weeds. Keep the soil moist but not too wet.

4 Carefully transfer your onions to a larger pot, spacing them out well. Water when the soil is dry and use a liquid feed once a month.

5 Pull back the soil around the swollen onion bulbs. Break off any flower stems that appear and stop watering when the bulbs begin to ripen.

6 Lift your onions out of the ground two weeks after the leaves turn yellow and flop over. You might need to use a garden fork.

Grow leeks in sunny places.

Leek
Grown for more than 6,000 years, leeks are thought to have been eaten by the ancient Egyptians, who built the pyramids.

Grow your own garlic
Place one clove, pointy end up, 5 cm (2 in) deep in a medium-sized pot and cover with a little soil. Always keep the soil moist. Break off all flower stems and stop watering in late summer. Lift in the same way as onions.

1 Make a hole 1.5 cm (½ in) deep with your finger or a pencil, and put in a few leek seeds. Cover with soil, and water. You can keep them outdoors.

2 Once the seedlings are growing healthily, water them well. Then make some holes 15 cm (6 in) deep in a large pot. Now, lift out the seedlings and carefully separate them.

3 Trim each leek's root ends to 2.5 cm (1 in) long with scissors. Then place each one into its own hole in the large pot.

4 Fill each hole with water. The soil washed in will hold each leek in place. Continue to water regularly and use a liquid feed once a month.

5 Get longer leeks by adding more soil to the pot, raising the soil level around the base of each leek.

6 Lift some baby leeks when small. You can leave other leeks in longer – even over winter – to grow bigger.

Eat it Onion and leek soup

Onions and leeks are great for adding flavour to savoury meals. They also contain vitamins and minerals that will help to keep your heart healthy.

You'll need

washed well — or vegetable stock

| 50 g (2 oz) butter | 4 leeks, trimmed and sliced | 1 large onion, chopped | 2 medium potatoes, chopped | 1 litre (1.7 pints) chicken stock | small bunch of tarragon, chopped | 250 ml (9 fl oz) milk | salt and pepper | crème fraîche |

Your eyes may water when peeling onions.

Onion pizza: see page 78

When fully grown, leeks need to be washed well to loosen any dirt between the leaves.

Leek seedling

1 Melt the butter in a large saucepan then add the onion and leeks. Cook gently for about 5-7 minutes until the onion and leeks are softened.

2 Add the potatoes and stock. Cook for a further 10 minutes or until the potatoes are tender.

3 Stir in the tarragon. Remove from heat and leave to cool. It is dangerous to blend a soup when hot as the heat will force off the lid of the blender.

4 Pour the cold mixture into a blender. Blend until smooth. Reheat with the milk in a saucepan to make soup. Season with salt and pepper.

5 **Serve the soup** in small bowls. Create a face with crème fraîche on the surface of each serving. Serve with slices of bread if you wish.

A warm, tasty soup for cold winter days.

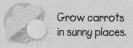

Carrots

Pulling up carrots is always a big surprise, because you won't know beforehand how big they'll be. The secret is to encourage good root growth, because this is the part we eat. There are many varieties and some take longer to grow than others.

1 Use a very deep container to give room for the long roots. Fill with soil-based potting compost. Sow carrots where they are to grow as they don't like being transplanted.

2 Sow seeds into a trench 1.5 cm (½ in) deep. Use your fingertips to cover the seeds with soil, then water and label. Keep outside from mid-spring.

3 Thin the germinated seedlings so they are 8 cm (3 in) apart. You can use these thinnings in salads or put them into your compost bin.

4 Water often so the roots don't split. But be careful not to over-water otherwise too much leaf will grow instead of the roots.

5 Lift some when small as baby carrots. Water before lifting so the other carrots are not disturbed.

6 Leave other carrots to get bigger and then pull up from the base of the stem. Use a garden fork to loosen the surrounding soil.

The first carrots were white, purple, red, yellow, green, or black. Long, orange carrots were developed in the 1500s by Dutch growers in honour of their royal family - the House of Orange.

Carrot pests can attack both the leaves and the roots of the plant.

Yuck, that leek stinks!

Companion planting
Sow leeks in with carrots. As they grow, they both have strong scents and may drive away each other's pests. This is called companion planting.

You'll need

Pre-heat 200°C, 400°F. Gas 6	140 g (5 oz) plain flour	85 g (3 oz) light brown sugar	100 g (4 oz) grated carrot	100 g (4 oz) porridge oats	½ tsp ground cinnamon	200 ml (7 fl oz) buttermilk *or milk + 1 tbsp lemon juice*	3 tbsp melted butter	bicarbonate of soda *2 tsp baking powder* *½ tsp*

chopped	chopped finely						Muffin topping	
50 g (2 oz) roasted hazelnuts	100 g (4 oz) unsulphured apricots	1 tbsp poppy seeds	zest of 2 oranges	1 egg, beaten	juice of 1 large orange	a pinch of salt	2 tbsp soft brown sugar	1 tbsp melted butter	50 g (2 oz) porridge oats

Carrots can be used in making both savoury meals or sweet cakes. Full of healthy goodness and vitamins, these delicious muffins are ideal for a party or a treat for your lunch box.

1 **To make** the topping, mix together the sugar, oats, and melted butter. Sprinkle the mixture onto a baking sheet. Bake for five minutes, then leave to cool.

2 **Mix the flour**, baking powder, bicarbonate of soda, and sugar. Add the nuts, carrot, apricots, poppy seeds, cinnamon, oats, and orange zest. Mix well.

3 **In another bowl**, use a spoon to mix the buttermilk, egg, butter, salt, and orange juice. Pour this onto the dry mixture.

4 **Stir the two mixtures** together using a spoon. Do not over mix as this will "knock out" all the air. The lumpier the mixture, the better the muffins will be!

5 **Place eight** paper cases into a muffin tray. Spoon the mixture into the cases, filling them two-thirds full.

6 **Sprinkle the crumbly** topping over the muffins. Bake them for about 25-30 minutes until well risen and golden. Leave to cool.

A perfect lunchbox treat!

Go to page 78 for another carrot recipe idea.

47

Grow spinach in a cool place, out of direct sunlight.

Spinach

All parts of the plants from the spinach family have been cooked or used in medicines since ancient times. The tasty leaves and nutritious leafstalks can help to keep us healthy and strong.

1 In a long, deep container, make a trench 2.5 cm (1 in) deep using a ruler. Sow spinach seeds thinly along the row from mid-spring.

2 Once germinated, thin the seedlings to 8 cm (3 in) apart and throw away the ones you have removed. Thin them again at a later stage if necessary.

5 Pick some outer leaves when longer than 5 cm (2 in). Encourage new growth by picking a few leaves often.

3 Keep well watered and use a liquid feed once a month. Add a nitrogen-rich fertilizer to the soil to add goodness.

4 Pinch out flowering shoots as they appear so that the plant can concentrate on producing good leaves.

Beetroot

There are white and yellow as well as red varieties of beetroot. Farmers grow sugar beets and then extract the sugar.

1 Make holes 2.5 cm (1 in) deep, spaced out around your large container. Sow two seeds into each hole. Cover with soil, water well, and put in a label.

2 Thin the germinated seedlings when they are 2.5 cm (1 in) high to one per hole. Throw away the seedlings that you have removed.

Twist off the tops using your hands. (Don't cut with a knife or the beetroot will "bleed".) These leaves can be cooked and eaten like spinach.

Do not grow the plants too close together or the roots will not grow very big.

3 Keep well watered as dry spells can cause the beetroots to become woody and split, and their growth stunted.

4 Beetroot is ready to pick when the size of a golf ball. Lift the beetroot holding the tops and using a fork to lever under the root.

Allow some others to grow bigger to the size of a tennis ball.

 You'll need

Here's a recipe to strengthen your muscles, boost your energy, and keep you healthy all thanks to the minerals and vitamins in spinach.

For the pastry

| 150 g (6 oz) wholemeal flour | 100 g (4 oz) plain flour | 125 g (5 oz) butter | 3 tbsp cold water, or less | a pinch of salt | 750 g (1 lb 10 oz) fresh spinach, trimmed | 2 egg yolks | 200 ml (7 fl oz) crème fraîche | 1 clove garlic, crushed | *nutmeg* freshly ground black pepper | *freshly grated* 50 g (2 oz) Parmesan |

1 **Rub the butter** into the flour until finely crumbed. Stir in the salt and add enough water to bring the mixture together into a ball. Roll out the pastry thinly.

Baking time 10 mins with beans, 5 mins without

2 **Cut out** 24 circles and press into bun tins. Place a piece of parchment paper into each pastry and fill with baking beans. Bake in the oven.

Cooking time 1-2 mins

3 **Wash the spinach** well then place in a large saucepan. Cover and cook until wilted, stirring once or twice. Wash under cold water until cool.

4 **Drain well,** then squeeze the spinach in a clean tea towel until as dry as possible. Chop roughly.

5 **In a bowl,** beat the egg yolks with the crème fraîche and garlic. Season with freshly grated nutmeg and pepper and stir in the spinach.

Baking time 15-20 mins

6 **Spoon out** the mixture evenly into pastry cases. Sprinkle Parmesan over the top of each tart. Bake in the oven until the filling has just set.

Plants protect themselves from pests by producing phytochemicals (fight-o-chemicals). When we eat them, the phytochemicals fight to keep us healthy, too. Spinach contains one called lutein, which keeps our eyes healthy.

Go to page 79 for another spinach recipe idea.

Lettuce

Flat or curly, green or purple – there are many varieties of crispy lettuce leaves. Sow the seeds at any time through the spring and summer, and end up with a long-lasting crop.

This funky lettuce is called Lollo Rosso.

1 In a pot full of seed compost, use a pencil to make a 1.5 cm (½ in) deep circular trench.

2 Take a pinch of the tiny seeds from a pile in your hand and sprinkle them along the trench in your pot.

3 Cover the seeds with soil, using your fingertips, then water the soil. Remember to label your pot with the variety of lettuce you have planted.

4 Once the seedlings start to germinate, pull out some to allow others to grow. Once it's a good size, transplant each lettuce into its own pot.

5 Put your pots on a high shelf and pour some gravel around the base of the lettuce to deter slugs and snails getting to the leaves.

6 Water often to keep the soil moist. This needs to be done once or twice a day during warm weather as the soil will dry out quickly.

Try using an old wooden crate for your crops. Line the crate with a waterproof plastic sheet, like a large bin bag, and fill with potting compost. Sow the seeds directly into the soil. The wood keeps in valuable warmth and moisture.

Mix your seeds for a colourful crop.

Pick the outer leaves as you need them, and your lettuce will keep growing more and more leaves for you.

53

You'll need

DRESSING

125 g (5 oz) silken tofu

2 tsp sesame oil

SALAD

mixed salad leaves

2 tbsp extra virgin olive oil

1 tbsp mustard seeds

CROUTONS

6 slices wholemeal bread

½ tbsp rice vinegar
1 tbsp soy sauce

1 tbsp mustard seeds

2 tbsp extra virgin olive oil

1 tbsp extra virgin olive oil

250 g (9 oz) fresh peas

Pre-heat

200°C, 400°F, Gas 6

1 tbsp runny honey

cut into strips
½ yellow, ½ orange peppers

1 tbsp water

12 cherry tomatoes, halved

2 tbsp

mint, chopped

very thin
2 carrots, 2 raw beetroot, cut in strips

salt and freshly ground black pepper

8 baby corn, cut in half lengthwise

1 tbsp sesame seeds

2 tbsp pumpkin seeds

Food is full of colour, and this healthy salad with a tofu dressing will bring dynamic colour to the table. A serving bowl with blue in its pattern will complete the rainbow.

Recipe idea: see page 79
Bulgar wheat salad

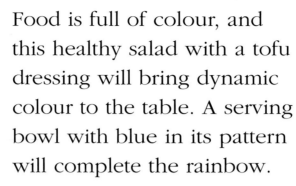

1 **Cut shapes** out of the bread, using cutters. Brush the bread with olive oil and bake in the oven for about five minutes until golden brown.

2 **Place all the** ingredients for the dressing in a blender. Blend until smooth. Season with salt and pepper according to your taste.

3 **Put the mixed leaves** in a colander and wash. Drain well. Make a large bed of the leaves in a colourful serving bowl.

4 **Scatter** the pepper strips, fresh peas, and tomato halves on top of the salad leaves.

Cooking time

2–3 mins

5 **Heat the olive oil** in a large frying pan and add the mustard seeds. Once they start to pop add the beetroot, carrot, and baby corn. Cook them until just tender then tip over the salad ingredients in the serving bowl. Drizzle the dressing over the salad.

Sprinkle with seeds and serve with croutons.

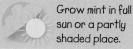

Grow mint in full
sun or a partly
shaded place.

Mint The leaves of a

mint plant are great for flavouring
food. You can grow mint from seed
or a cutting from a friend's mint plant.
The cutting method is called propagating.

One way to
grow mint is to
cut off a branch
from a mint plant,
strip the lower
leaves, and place
the stem in a
bottle of water.
Watch for the
roots to grow
and then plant.

1 **In autumn or winter,**
dig up part of a mint plant.
Cut off a few good roots. Return
the plant to its place.

2 **For each cutting,** make
a straight cut where the root
was attached to the parent plant.
This is the top of the root.

4 **Fill a pot** with moist soil.
Make some deep holes with
a pencil. Place each root into a
hole. The top end should be level
with the surface of the soil.

5 **Cover the surface** with
grit to push the soil down.
Do not water. Watch and wait for
the new plants to grow.

Mint has a very strong scent, which is said to repel aphids and other pests. So, mint can be a companion plant.

1 **In early spring,** make some holes in the bottom of a container, such as a clear plastic egg box. Fill the container with moist soil or compost. Sprinkle the mint seeds very thinly onto the surface of the soil.

3 **Make a sloping cut** a short distance along the root. This is the bottom of the root.

2 **Close the lid** of the plastic egg box, or cover the container, to keep the seeds warm. During germination, keep the soil moist but not very wet.

3 **Lift out** a section of the seedlings when they have germinated and plant them into a larger pot.

6 **Plant the mint** cuttings into their own pots once the plants have grown good roots. Water to keep the soil moist.

4 **Water often** during the summer to keep the soil moist. Mint will grow and spread quickly. The young, tender leaves are ready to pick and use.

5 **Pick the growing tip** so the plant will become bushy. These leaves can be used for cooking. The plant will die back in autumn and re-grow in spring.

Eat it Chocolate and mint mousse

You'll need

chopped

290 ml (10 fl oz) double cream

small bunch of mint

125 ml (4 fl oz) milk

small pieces

175 g (7 oz) dark chocolate

3 egg yolks

1 ½ tbsp golden icing sugar

cocoa powder for dusting

Pre-heat

150°C, 275°F, Gas 3

Tickle your tastebuds with the flavour of mint. Throw a leaf or two into a pan of potatoes or peas, or into a glass of hot water for a refreshing tea, or into this mousse.

More mint recipes

Mint sauce: see page 79

Mint tea: see page 79

Why not make minty ice cubes by adding mint leaves to the water before freezing?

1 **Pour the cream** into a small pan. Add the chopped mint. Heat gently until nearly boiling, then remove from heat, cover, and leave for 30 minutes.

2 **Meanwhile,** pour the milk into another small pan and heat gently. Remove from heat and stir in the chocolate until it has melted and the mixture is smooth.

3 **Whisk the egg yolks** and sugar together and add the chocolate milk and the minty cream. Mix well, then strain the mixture through a fine sieve.

Baking time 45–60 mins

4 **Pour the mixture** into four ramekins or heat-proof cups. Stand the cups in a roasting tin. Add hot water until it's halfway up the outside of the cups. Bake.

Sooo chocolatey, sooo minty!

5 **While the puddings** are completely cooling in a fridge, make a stencil from a piece of card. Cut out different-sized holes in the card. Before serving each chocolate mousse, hold the stencil over the top and sprinkle through some cocoa powder.

59

Sunflower

As bright as the Sun, these brilliant yellow flowers will stand out amongst your fruit and vegetables. But wait before picking, because it's the seeds you are after for eating.

Recycle newspapers by rolling them up to make biodegradable pots.

1 At the end of spring, put soil into some small pots with holes in their base. Use your finger to make a hole 2.5 cm (1 in) deep in each pot.

2 Sow one seed into each hole. Cover the seeds lightly with soil. Water and place the pot onto a sunny windowsill.

3 Cover the pot with a see-through polythene bag to keep in the heat. Remove this bag when the leaves appear on the seedlings.

4 Keep watering little but often. Watch and wait. They'll be ready to plant outside when they are large enough to handle and their roots fill the pot.

5 When a seedling has outgrown its pot, it is ready to plant into a large container. Scoop out a pot-sized hole and carefully place the seedling into it. Water in.

6 Once the plant is bigger, push a cane a short distance away from the main stem. Use string to tie the stem, loosely to the cane. As it grows, make a tie every 20 cm (8 in).

Before opening, the flower bud will follow the position of the Sun through the day.

7 Continue to water little but often, as without water, the sunflower will quickly wither. Keep the plant free from pests by picking them off with your fingers.

8 Use a measuring tape to find out the height of your sunflower. You could make a chart to see how quickly it grows.

Wait for the flower heads to turn brown, then tap out the seeds.

61

Eat it
Sunflower pot loaves

Fill your kitchen with the homely smell of bread-making. Also, why not try roasting sunflower seeds to munch as a snack?

You'll need

| 250 g (9 oz) strong white bread flour | 150 g (6 oz) wholemeal flour | 1 tsp salt | 1 tsp sugar | 1 sachet 7 g (½ oz) fast-action yeast | 250 ml (9 fl oz) warm water | 2 tbsp extra-virgin olive oil | 100 g (4 oz) sunflower seeds | four 11 x 10 cm (5 x 4 in) terracotta pots | a little milk | Pre-heat 200°C, 400°F, Gas 6 |

Baking time 35-40 mins

1 Scrub the flower pots with clean water. Oil the pots inside and out and bake them in a preheated oven. Let them cool. Repeat this process twice more.

2 Place the flour, salt, sugar, and yeast into a large bowl. Make a well in the centre and pour in the water and olive oil. Mix to make a soft but firm dough.

3 Turn the dough out onto a lightly dusted work surface and knead well for at least 10 minutes. Swap over with an adult if your arms are getting tired.

4 Make a dip and add three-quarters of the sunflower seeds. Knead them into the dough.

You can leave the dough to rise overnight in the fridge.

5 Divide the dough into four pieces and place one ball into each flower pot. Cover the pots with a plastic bag and leave until the dough has doubled in size.

Cooking time 35-40 mins

6 Brush the tops of the risen loaves with a little milk. Sprinkle over the remaining sunflower seeds and bake the loaves in the oven until golden.

62

Go to page 19 for another sunflower-seed recipe idea.

Slip me out of the pot and look what you've got!

63

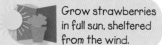
Strawberries

Follow the steps below and you will have delicious red strawberries to enjoy eating in the summer, year after year.

You can buy strawberry plugs from most garden centres or a mail-order supplier, who will send them in a box.

1 **The easiest way** to grow strawberry plants is to start off with strawberry plugs. The neat root ball makes the plugs easy to plant and quick to get growing.

2 **Place the plug** into a hole in a medium-sized pot. The top of the roots, called the "crown", should be level with the top of the soil. Water the soil well.

3 **Put straw under** the plant to stop the strawberries lying on the ground. This also keeps the soil warm and stops the plant losing moisture.

4 **Water young plants** every day. Once the plant is flowering, feed every 10 days until the strawberries are ready to pick.

Make more plants

Strawberry plants form runners during the growing season. In late summer, when the new plants along the runners have some roots, cut them from the parent plant. Leave about 5 cm (2 in) of runner each side of the new plants.

Straight away, replant each one, by pegging the ends down with garden wire or u-shaped staples. Take care of these new plants as you did for the parent plant.

5 **Check every other** day to see if any strawberries have turned red. As soon as one is ripe, pick straight away, so that it doesn't rot. Make sure the green stalk stays on until the strawberry is eaten.

A strawberry is not really a fruit but the swollen base of the flower. There are about 200 seeds on the outer skin of each strawberry.

You may also want to cover your plant with netting to stop birds eating the strawberries.

Water often as the strawberries begin to swell.

Place the pot on a table, or put broken eggshells or grit under each plant to deter slugs getting to them.

Eat it — Strawberry meringue

Add colour and flavour to cakes and desserts with your fresh and juicy-red strawberries. Sliced, blended, or eaten whole, they'll go down a treat.

You'll need

 3 egg whites

 a pinch of salt

 100 g (4 oz) caster sugar

 25 g (1oz) dark chocolate

 500 g (1 lb) fresh strawberries

1 tbsp golden icing sugar

250 ml (9 fl oz) whipping cream

Pre-heat 120°C, 250°F, Gas 1

1 Pour the egg whites and salt into a bowl and whisk until stiff and soft peaks form. Mix in the caster sugar a spoonful at a time to make the meringue mixture.

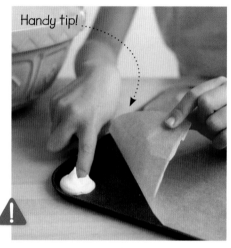

Handy tip!

2 Place a splodge of meringue mixture at each corner of a baking tray and lay a piece of baking sheet on top. This will keep the sheet still.

3 Melt the chocolate in a heat-proof bowl set over a saucepan of simmering water. Dribble a few spoonfuls of the melted chocolate over the mixture.

Cooking time 4 hrs

4 Scoop large spoonfuls of the swirly meringue onto the baking sheet. Keep dribbling more chocolate into the bowl. Put the filled tray into the oven.

Whizz till smoooooth!

5 Make the sauce while the meringues are cooling on a wire rack. Do this by placing half the strawberries and the icing sugar into a blender and whizzing.

6 Whip the cream until soft, using a whisk. To serve, place a meringue on a plate and dollop a spoonful of cream over the top . . .

7 ...**Scatter over a** handful of sliced strawberries and then pour over the strawberry sauce, using a spoon. Now enjoy!

Top tip:
For a low-sugar strawberry sauce, replace the golden icing sugar with runny honey.

More strawberry recipes

Strawberry mousse: see page 79

Strawberry pancakes: see page 79

Strawberry fondue: see page 79

Pick and eat!
You don't have to wait to taste your strawberries. Give them a wash and you can try them straightaway.

Blueberries

Blueberry bushes grow well in pots filled with acidic (or "ericaceous") soil. Care for them year after year and you'll be rewarded with loads of fruit.

How to begin?
You can either buy a young blueberry plant or one already brimming with fruit or flowers. If you plant two or more together, 1 m (3 ft) apart, then you'll get better fruit year after year.

1 m (3 ft)

In pots, blueberry bushes grow best filled with a mixture of ericaceous compost and peat.

1 Fill your large pot with compost mixture. Make a large hole and carefully drop in your blueberry plant. Add some more compost around the plant. Press down to make it stand firm.

2 Mulch around the new plant using bark or pine needles, which are fairly acidic. Do this again each spring.

3 Cover with netting, if your new plant already has some berries. This will stop birds from eating the berries.

4 Water the new plant in well using rainwater. (Tap water will make the soil less acidic.) Continue to water your plant often from spring to autumn.

Blueberries form on branches that grew in the previous year. To get the best berries, plants over three years old must be pruned each year, sometime between winter and spring.

Before pruning

After pruning

When pruning, remove any dead or diseased branches and cut off at the base one or two of the oldest branches that aren't producing much. This will make room for the younger branches and give you a good crop next time.

Blueberries form in clusters, but ripen at different times. Pick each berry a few days after it turns a deep blue colour and easily pulls away.

Eat it Blueberry cheesecake

By the end of the summer, your blueberries will be ripe for picking. Try eating them fresh with cream or yoghurt, or add them to muffin mixes or smoothies.

You'll need

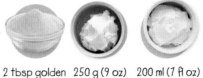

| 500 g (1 lb) blueberries | 2 tbsp golden caster sugar | 250 g (9 oz) cream cheese | 200 ml (7 fl oz) crème fraîche | ¼ tsp vanilla extract | 8 oat biscuits, crushed |

More blueberry recipes

Pancakes: see page 79

Smoothie: see page 79

Muffins: see page 79

1 **Place ¾ of the berries** and ½ the sugar into a small saucepan. Cover and simmer for five minutes until soft. Stir in the other berries and leave to cool.

2 **Using a wooden spoon,** beat the cream cheese, crème fraîche, remaining sugar, and vanilla extract together in a mixing bowl. Continue until well mixed and soft.

3 **Fill four glasses** with a spoonful of the blueberry sauce, then a spoonful of the cream-cheese mixture, and then a spoonful of crushed biscuits.

4 **Repeat the layers** once more and then put the filled glasses in the fridge for an hour.

Go to page 79 for more blueberry recipe ideas.

The blueberry is one of the few fruits native to North America. Some native Americans call it a star berry because the white flowers are shaped like five-pointed stars.

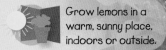
Lemon

All-year-round care for your lemon plant will reward you with a healthy, pretty tree bearing lots of lemons. Cover your tree in winter to protect from frost and give it a special feed every month from early spring to late summer.

Growing from seed

As long as a lemon seed has not been damaged, it could grow into a lemon tree.

Select the seeds that are whole and undamaged. Sow them while they are still moist.

Cut a lemon in half and remove the seeds.

Lemon seed

Have patience! It's likely to take eight years or more before your plants flower and bear fruit.

Growing from a young tree

1 **Buy a lemon tree** that is ready to begin fruiting. Place it upright in a pot filled with citrus compost. Add more compost if needed to help the tree stand firm.

2 **Add 5 cm (2 in) mulch** around the trunk to keep in moisture and warmth. Newly planted trees need watering often to begin with.

3 **As the tree grows,** water very well only when the topsoil looks dry. During the winter, the tree will need less watering.

Lemons contain the most vitamin C of any citrus fruit. In the past, sailors ate them on voyages to stay healthy and quench their thirst.

From flower to fruit

Watch out for the lemon tree's sharp thorns!

The first flower buds will begin appearing in late spring.

Brilliant white flowers open to attract insects, such as bees, to take pollen from one flower to another.

Fruits form from pollinated flowers, turning from green to yellow as they swell.

Lemonade lollies

Keep cool on a hot summer's day with the zingy taste of your juicy lemons. Lemons add flavour to fish and salads as well.

Add slices of lemon to drinks and salads.

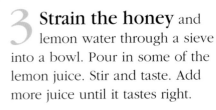

You'll need

18 lolly sticks

6 juicy lemons

250 ml (8 fl oz) runny honey

700ml (25 fl oz) cold water

18 empty yoghurt pots

1 Finely grate the zest from three of the lemons and place in a pan with the honey and 500 ml (18 fl oz) water. Bring to the boil, then remove from heat.

2 Squeeze the juice from all of the lemons. Pour into a jug. This should give you about 200-250 ml (7-8 fl oz) of juice.

3 Strain the honey and lemon water through a sieve into a bowl. Pour in some of the lemon juice. Stir and taste. Add more juice until it tastes right.

Freezing time 1-2 hours

4 Leave the lemonade to cool in the fridge. Add the rest of the water to dilute. Stir, then pour into 18 empty yoghurt pots. Place in the freezer until partly set.

5 Push a lolly stick into each pot. Return the pots to the freezer until the lemonade becomes completely solid.

6 Crunch! Enjoy the cold juicy taste, but be quick as your lolly will quickly start to melt on a warm day.

Throw in some ice cubes. Sooo cool!

For a refreshing drink, pour a little of your lemonade (from Step 3) into a glass and top up with cold fizzy water.

Many of the plants you have grown have produced seeds, which you could collect and then use next year. The secret of success is to collect the seeds at the right time and store them in the right way.

Sunflower seeds

can be collected when the seed heads look big, fat, and brown. Cut off the whole seed head, put into a paper bag, and shake or pinch out the seeds.

Brilliant, bargain beans

1 Choose a healthy plant. Wait until the seed heads or seedpods have ripened and are about to split. Then, on a dry, windless day, cut off the entire seed head or pod.

Store seeds in a paper bag

2 Remove the seeds using your fingers. In a warm place, leave the seeds to dry on a piece of kitchen towel. Label and store the seeds in a dry, cool place until spring.

3 Prepare a pot ready for sowing your seeds. Some seeds that are very dried out may need soaking first to encourage them to swell and germinate.

4 Last year's seeds have become this year's new plant. Why not trade seeds with other gardeners and give some to your friends to have a go, too?

Onion seed heads　　Lettuce run to seed　　Fresh bean seeds　　Corn flowers　　Seeds scattering

Make a seed-box organizer

Your seeds need looking after while being stored, so what better way to keep them cool, dry, and safe than in your own seed box. If you organize them carefully, you'll know at a glance when to sow them next year.

1 **Find a box** and a lid and wrap them in colourful paper. Cut out some season dividers from cardboard.

2 **Paint a colourful design** on the dividers. When dry, write SPRING SUMMER, and AUTUMN on them to show when to sow the seeds next year.

3 **Decorate small envelopes** using colourful paints. Also, you could draw or stick on your own plant pictures. Once the envelope is dry, put the seeds inside.

Dwarf french beans

Collected on 14th August 2007

Sow in spring

4 **Seal the envelopes** and label them with the name of the fruit or vegetable, its variety, and the date. Place in the organizer and cover with the lid.

SUMMER

Sun

SPRING

Runner beans

Courgette seeds

Tomato sauce

Warm the oil in a large pan over moderate heat. Add the onion and garlic, cover, and cook for about four minutes until the mixture is soft but not browned. Add the tomatoes, reduce the heat, cover, and cook for about 15 minutes until the tomatoes have collapsed. Remove from heat. Cool, then puree the mixture in a food processor or blender. Pass through a sieve. Use on pizzas or reheat before serving.

- 1 tbsp olive oil
- 1 small onion, finely chopped
- 1 garlic glove, finely chopped
- 1 kg (2 lb) whole ripe tomatoes

Ratatouille

Sprinkle salt over the aubergine and courgette slices in a bowl, press down with a plate, and leave for one hour. Plunge the tomatoes in a bowl of boiling water for a few minutes, then skin them, quarter them, remove the seeds, and slice. Warm oil in a large pan. Fry onions and garlic for 10 minutes, then add peppers. Rinse the courgettes and aubergines and dry with kitchen paper. Add courgettes, aubergines, and basil to the mixture and season. Stir, cover, and then simmer for 30 minutes. Add tomato flesh and cook for a further 15 minutes with the lid off. Use as a side dish or as a jacket-potato filling.

- 3 courgettes, sliced
- 2 aubergines, sliced
- 2 onions chopped
- 5 ripe tomatoes
- 2 red or green peppers, cored and chopped
- 2 garlic cloves, crushed
- 4 tbsp olive oil
- 1 tbsp basil
- salt and pepper

Stuffed courgettes

Halve the courgettes and blanch in boiling water for 3-4 minutes. Drain and cool. Scoop out seeds and a little flesh (to use later). Place courgettes in a greased dish. Warm the oil in a small pan. Add onion and red pepper, cover, and cook until soft. Add garlic, thyme, courgette flesh, and season with pepper. Stir the mixture and then spoon into the courgette halves. Bake for 15 minutes.

- 4 courgettes
- 2 tbsp olive oil
- 1 onion, chopped
- 2 red peppers, cored and diced
- 2 garlic cloves, chopped
- 2 tbsp thyme
Preheat oven 180°C, 350°F, Gas 4

Pumpkin bread

Line a loaf tin with baking parchment. Sift the flour, baking powder, salt, cinnamon, and nutmeg into a bowl and make a hole in the middle. Mix the pumpkin, eggs, oil, and sugars. Pour ¾ of this mixture into the hole. Mix with a spoon, then stir in the remaining pumpkin mixture until smooth. Pour into the tin and bake for 55-60 minutes until the loaf begins to shrink from the sides. Cool slightly, then turn out onto a wire rack to cool completely.

- 180 g (6 oz) strong white flour
- 1 tsp baking powder
- 1 tsp ground cinnamon
- ½ tsp salt
- ¼ tsp ground nutmeg
- 180 ml (6 fl oz) pumpkin puree (see p. 30)
- 2 eggs beaten
- 60 ml (2 fl oz) oil
- 100 g (4 oz) caster sugar
- 50 g (2 oz) brown sugar
Preheat oven 180°C, 350°F, Gas 4

Bean omelette

Heat the oil in a frying pan. Cook the onion, pepper, and beans gently until soft. Add the potato and cook for two minutes. Beat the eggs in a bowl. Stir in the onions, pepper, beans, and potatoes, and season with pepper. Melt the butter in a frying pan. Pour the mixture into the pan. Cook over a low heat for about 10 minutes, then brown the top under the grill.

- 1 large onion, finely chopped
- 1 large red pepper, diced
- 150 g (6 oz) green beans, chopped finely
- 2 medium cooked potatoes, sliced
- 2 tbsp olive oil
- 4 eggs
- 2 tbsp butter

Onion pizza

Boil the onions for six minutes, drain and cool. Thinly slice the onions. Sprinkle olive oil over the pizza base, then spread over the onions. Sprinkle on the cheese and herbs and season with salt and pepper. Bake in the oven for 25 minutes. Chop the parsley and sprinkle over the pizza. Serve.

- Pizza base
- 3 medium onions
- 3 tbsp parsley
- 2 tbsp olive oil
- 25 g (1 oz) romano cheese
- 50 g (2 oz) mozzarella cheese
- 1 tsp mixed herbs
Preheat oven 220°C, 425°F, Gas 7

Jacket-potato mice

Wash potatoes and dry with paper towel. Prick with a fork and place on a baking tray. Cook for 60-75 minutes until soft inside and skins crisp. Remove from oven. Cut each potato in half and scoop out the soft insides into a mixing bowl. Place the skins back on the baking tray. Mash the potato well, add butter and seasoning, and spoon back into the skins. Sprinkle the cheese over the potatoes and cook in the oven for a further 15 minutes. For each potato, press on two radish halves for the ears, chives for the whiskers, a tomato for the nose, raisins for the eyes, and a spring onion for the tail.

- 4 large potatoes
- 50 g (2 oz) butter
- salt and pepper
- 125 g (5 oz) Cheddar cheese, grated
- 4 radish, halved
- 4 cherry tomatoes
- chives, chopped in sticks
- 8 raisins
- 2 spring onions, halved
Preheat oven 200°C, 400°F, Gas 6

Carrot soup

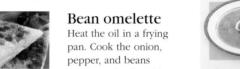

Put the carrots, garlic, zest, orange juice, and water in a pan. Cover and simmer for 20 minutes until the carrots are soft. Let the soup cool then add nutmeg and lemon juice. Pour into a blender and blend until smooth. Return the soup to the pan, stir in the cream, and season with pepper. Then reheat the soup without letting it boil.

- 6 carrots, peeled and sliced
- 2 cloves garlic, peeled
- zest of 1 orange, grated
- juice of 1 lemon
- 300 ml (11 fl oz) water
- pinch of ground nutmeg
- 300 ml (11 fl oz) orange juice
- 300 ml (11 fl oz) light cream

Beetroot salad

Trim and scrub the beetroot, then place in a pan and cover with slightly salty water. Bring to the boil and cook the beetroot for about 30 minutes until a knife can pass through easily. Drain well and skin when cool enough to handle. Slice into pieces, sprinkle over the pieces of orange peel, and serve.

- home-grown beetroot
- a pinch of salt
- orange peel, sliced finely

Spinach gnocchi

To make the sauce, warm the oil in a frying pan. Add onion, carrot, and celery and cook for 10 minutes. Add the tomatoes, season, and simmer for 25-35 minutes, stirring occasionally until the sauce thickens. Pour into a blender and puree. To make the dough, boil the potatoes until tender, drain well, and then mash. Boil the spinach for two minutes, drain, and then chop finely. Mix the potatoes and the spinach with the flour to form a dough. Knead the dough on a floured board. Divide into 12 pieces and roll each piece into a long cylinder. Cut into 2 cm (¾ in) pieces to make gnocchi. Boil the pieces for two minutes, drain well, and place in a greased baking dish. Reheat the sauce, stir in the cream, season, and spoon over the gnocchi. Bake for 5-7 minutes. Garnish with parsley before serving.

For the dough:
- 500 g (1 lb) potatoes, peeled
- 125 g (5 oz) fresh spinach
- 75 g (3 oz) plain flour

For the sauce:
- 1 tbsp oil
- 1 small onion
- 1 small carrot
- 1 celery stick
- 5 tomatoes, peeled, deseeded, chopped
- 125 ml (4 fl oz) double cream
- pepper to season
- sprigs of parsley, chopped
Preheat oven 220°C, 425°F, Gas 7

Bulgar-wheat salad

Soak the bulgar in a bowl of boiling water for 20 minutes until the grains soften. Drain the bulgar in a sieve over a bowl and squeeze out any extra water with your hands. Combine all the ingredients, mix together, and season with pepper. Arrange the washed lettuce leaves on a serving bowl and then pour the bulgar mixture on top.

- lettuce leaves,
- 175 g (7 oz) bulgar
- ½ cucumber, finely chopped
- 4 spring onions, finely sliced
- 1 bunch parsley, chopped
- handful of mint leaves, chopped
- 3 tbsp olive oil

Mint tea

Put tea and mint leaves in a teapot. Pour boiling water over the leaves. Stand for three minutes. Strain the tea before serving. Serve with a leaf or two of mint and a slice of lemon. Sweeten with honey if needed.

For each cup:
- ½ tsp tea leaves
- ½ tsp crushed mint leaves
- 1 cup boiling water
- sprig of mint
- slice of lemon
- tsp honey

Mint sauce

Place the mint and sugar into a jug and pour over the boiling water. Stir and leave to cool. Add vinegar and mix well. Add more water or vinegar and season to suit taste.

- Bunch of mint leaves, chopped finely
- 4 tbsp boiling water
- 4 tbsp white wine vinegar
- 1 tbsp caster sugar

Sunflower salad

Peel and grate the carrot. Toast the sunflower seeds lightly under the grill for a few minutes. Put the dressing ingredients into a jar, screw on a lid, and shake well. Put the carrot, sunflower seeds, and raisins into a salad bowl. Pour the dressing over the top. Toss the salad using two spoons. Season with salt and pepper if wish.

- 6 large carrots,
- 1 tbsp sunflower seeds
- 85 g (3 oz) raisins

For the dressing:
- juice from ½ orange
- juice from ½ lemon
- 1 tsp honey
- 3 tbsp olive oil
- ¼ tsp French mustard

Pancakes

Sieve flour and salt into a bowl. Make a "well" in the centre, add the egg and half the milk. Beat together and gradually mix into the flour until smooth. Beat in the rest of the milk and pour into a jug. Heat the pan over a medium heat. Add a teaspoon of butter or oil and swirl around. Pour two tablespoons of batter into pan, and tilt back and forth so the batter coats the base evenly. After 30 seconds, lift the edge of the pancake with a spatula to see if it is brown underneath. Loosen round the edges and flip the pancake. A few seconds later, slide the pancake out of the pan and onto a warm plate. Stack pancakes between layers of baking paper. Cover with foil to keep warm. Or, serve immediately and sprinkle with strawberry slices and a dollop of cream. Fold the pancake over.

For 10 pancakes:
- 100g (4 oz) plain flour
- pinch of salt
- 1 egg, beaten
- 300 ml (11 fl oz) milk
- 10 tsp butter or olive oil

For filling:
- strawberry slices and whipped cream

Alternative pancake filling:
- freshly squeezed lemon juice and caster sugar

Alternative:
- Add 50 g (2 oz) blueberries and 2 tbsp sugar into batter mixture. To serve, pour on maple syrup

Strawberry mousse

In a large bowl, whisk the cream and sugar until soft peaks form. Stir in the lemon juice to thicken. Mash the strawberries, then fold into the mixture. Spoon into four serving glasses.

- 100 g (4 oz) strawberries
- 3 tbsp sugar
- 220 ml (8 fl oz) double cream
- juice of 1 lemon

Strawberry fondue

Put the cream and chocolate in a saucepan. Over a low heat, stir the mixture until the chocolate has melted. Pour into the fondue pot. Dip the strawberries into the pot using fondue forks.

- 200 g (8 oz) plain or milk chocolate
- 80 ml (3 fl oz) double cream
- strawberries

Blueberry smoothie

Put all the ingredients into a blender. Add caster sugar if required. Cover and blend until smooth. Pour into glasses and serve.

- 1 small banana
- 150 g (6 oz) blueberries
- 300 ml (11 fl oz) milk

Blueberry muffins

Whisk the butter and sugar until fluffy. Still whisking, add the eggs one at a time. Add the vanilla extract and milk. Fold in the flour and a teaspoon of baking powder to make thick batter. Add the blueberries. Spoon the mixture into 12 paper muffin cases on a muffin tray. Bake for 30 minutes.

- 100 g (4 oz) caster sugar
- 100 g (4 oz) butter
- 300 g (12 oz) flour
- 2 eggs, beaten
- 140 ml (5 fl oz) milk
- 1 tsp vanilla extract
- 150 g (6 oz) blueberries
Preheat oven 160°C, 300°F, Gas 4

Lemon sorbet

Cut the tops off four lemons, scoop out the flesh and place the skins in the freezer. Put the lemon flesh, sugar, and water in a saucepan. Bring to the boil and simmer for five minutes. Strain the mixture and cool. Puree in a food processor until smooth. Scoop into the frozen lemon skins and freeze in an airtight container until ready to serve.

- 400 g (16 oz) sugar
- 300 ml (11 fl oz) water
- 6 lemons

Index

autumn 14, 37, 57, 68
  leaves 14, 15

biodegradable 6, 40, 60

companion planting 5, 19, 45, 57
compost 5, 6, 14, 15, 44, 68
  citrus compost 72
  compost bin 14, 15
  ericaceous compost 68
  potting compost 44, 53
  seed compost 20, 52
crock 7, 36

garden bugs 5, 14, 15
  aphids 5, 19, 32, 57
  bees 10
  birds 5, 65, 68
  ladybirds 5
  slugs 5, 32, 52, 65
  snails 5, 52
germination 10, 20, 28, 40, 44, 48, 49, 57, 76

leaf mould 15
lolly-stick labels 9

medicines 48
minerals 42, 50
mulch 15, 29, 32, 68, 72

nitrogen-rich fertilizer 48
nutrients 5, 14, 15

photosynthesis 11
pollination 12-13, 20, 24, 28, 73
propagating 56
protein 33
pruning 69

raised bed 7

seed-box organizer 77
spring 28, 40, 44, 48, 52, 57, 60, 68, 72, 73
stone markers 8
summer 28, 40, 41, 52, 64, 70, 72, 74

vegetable peelings 14
vitamins 42, 46, 50, 73

weeds 15, 36, 40
winter 36, 41, 43, 72
wooden crate 53

Suppliers

DK would like to thank:

Delfand Nurseries Ltd.
Wholesale; Nursery shop; Mail order suppliers.
Benwick Road, Doddington, March, Cambs. PE15 0TU
Tel: 01354 740553
www.organicplants.co.uk

Garsons
Farm Shop; Pick Your Own.
Winterdown Road, West End, Esher, Surrey KT10 8LS
Address to go here
Tel: 01372 464389
www.garsons.co.uk

Roots and Shoots
Wild Garden; Study Centre
Walnut Tree Walk
London SE11 6DN
Tel: 020 7587 1131
www.rootsandshoots.org.uk

The Garlic Farm
Newchurch, Isle of Wight
Tel: 01983 865378
www.thegarlicfarm.co.uk

Brockwell Park Community Greenhouses
Brixton, London

Antonia Salt at Green Ink
Garden Design Practice
www.greeninkgardens.com

Keift & Sons Ltd.
Quality flower bulbs
Tel: 01603 868911
www.kieftbulbs.co.uk

Alleyn Park Garden Centre Ltd.
Rear of 77 Park Hall Road, London SE21 8ES
Tel: 020 8670 7788
www.alleynpark.co.uk

Acknowledgements

DK would like to thank:

Vauxhall City Farm
Urban farm; Community garden.
165 Tyers Street, London SE11 5HS
Tel: 020 7582 4202
E-mail: vcf@btconnect.com
Director: Sharon Clouston
Community gardener:
Bernadette Kennedy

Staff and volunteers from VCF; and Diane Sullock, responsible for the community dye garden

With thanks to VCF for the use of their garden and for taking care of our plants.

DK Team
Sadie Thomas,
Deborah Lock,
Sonia Whillock-Moore

Photographer
Will Heap
www.willheap.com

Food Stylist
Annie Nichols
Annieisonthebeach Ltd.

Models Stanley and Scarlet Heap, Fiona Lock, Hannah and Max Moore, Matthew Morley, Jamie Chang-Leng, Spencer Britton, Kitty Nallet, Saphira Noor, Cara Crosby-Irons, Alfred and Molly Warren.

Picture credits

The publisher would like to thank the following for their kind permission to reproduce their photographs:

(Key: a-above; b-below/bottom; c-centre; l-left; r-right; t-top)

Alamy Images: Blickwinkel/Schmidbauer 12c; Blickwinkel/tomcook 68bl, 68cl; Creon Co.Ltd 75tl, 77fbr; Tim Gainey 70ftl; Andrea Jones 7fcla; MShieldsPhotos 73l; **Corbis:** J.Hall/photocuisine 76cb; **Flickr.com:** 4cr, 6fcr, 7c; John Barnabus 6tr; Buena Vida 60cr; Elemmakil 72c; Vanessa Evans 52ftr; Jomp Agullet 60tr; Mearse 6cr; Ken B. Miller 72cra; Tweetie Bird 73tr; **GAP Photos:** Visions 69c; **Getty Images:** Visuals Unlimited/John Gerlach 68tl; **Photolibrary:** Juliette H Wade/Espalier Media Ltd 53tr; **Photoshot / NHPA:** Stephen Dalton 45cb; **PunchStock:** BananaStock 14cb; **Science Photo Library:** B. W. Hoffman/Agstockusa 10-11c.

All other images © Dorling Kindersley
For further information see: www.dkimages.com